C O R E

REDEEMED

TURNING BROKENNESS INTO
SOMETHING BEAUTIFUL

ZONDERVAN™

ZONDERVAN

CORE for Men: Redeemed
Copyright © 2021 by CORE Ministries Inc.

Requests for information should be addressed to:

Zondervan, 3900 Sparks Drive SE, Grand Rapids, Michigan 49546

Scripture quotations marked ESV are taken from the ESV® Bible (The Holy Bible, English Standard Version®). Copyright © 2001 by Crossway, a publishing ministry of Good News Publishers. Used by permission. All rights reserved.

Scripture quotations marked NASB are taken from the New American Standard Bible®. Copyright © 1960, 1962, 1963, 1968, 1971, 1972, 1973, 1975, 1977, 1995 by The Lockman Foundation. Used by permission. (www.Lockman.org).

Scripture quotations marked NIV are taken from The Holy Bible, New International Version®, NIV®. Copyright © 1973, 1978, 1984, 2011 by Biblica, Inc.® Used by permission of Zondervan. All rights reserved worldwide. www.Zondervan.com. The "NIV" and "New International Version" are trademarks registered in the United States Patent and Trademark Office by Biblica, Inc.®

Scripture quotations marked NKJV is [are] taken from the New King James Version®. © 1982 by Thomas Nelson. Used by permission. All rights reserved.

Scripture quotations marked NLT are taken from the Holy Bible, New Living Translation. © 1996, 2004, 2007, 2013, 2015 by Tyndale House Foundation. Used by permission of Tyndale House Publishers, Inc., Carol Stream, Illinois 60188. All rights reserved.

Any internet addresses (websites, blogs, etc.) and telephone numbers in this book are offered as a resource. They are not intended in any way to be or imply an endorsement by Zondervan, nor does Zondervan vouch for the content of these sites and numbers for the life of this book.

Published in association with The Fedd Agency, 401 Ranch Road 620 South, Suite 250, Austin, TX 78734.

ISBN 978-0-310-13161-8 (softcover)

ISBN 978-0-310-13162-5 (ebook)

First Printing January 2021 / Printed in the United States of America

WE WOULD LIKE TO THANK:

Kris Kile, whose wisdom and labor is reflected throughout this entire guide. Without Kris's contributions, this series would not be what it is.

Jeff, for his ability to help us make this guide less informational and more conversational.

Jesse and his team at OX Creative, for the beautifully creative ways that they shaped the look and feel of this project.

Dean, for his courage, friendship, and sacrificial financial partnership.

CORE Ministries, Inc.
PO Box 93007
Austin TX 78709

COREUNITES.COM

Contents

DISCUSSION GUIDE · PERSONAL STUDY · SCRIPTURE REFLECTION

IT IS NEVER
TOO LATE
TO BE WHAT
YOU MIGHT
HAVE BEEN.

George Eliot

WE ARE EXCITED YOU CHOSE TO BE A PART OF THIS JOURNEY.

We have been working with men in stadiums, arenas, churches, businesses, and homes for decades and can sum up what we have seen as their biggest battles in two words: *Isolation* and *Disqualification*.

- **Isolation: "If you knew how messed up some of my life is, you wouldn't want to have anything to do with me."**
- **Disqualification: "If you knew how messed up some of my life is, you wouldn't want me to have anything to do with you."**

The passion behind CORE is to create spaces where men have permission to be real. Spaces where men discover they are not alone with the kind of doubts and fears they face. Spaces where they have like-minded brothers who are there with them.

In spite of what our culture might tell us, **life was not designed to figure things out on our own.** When Jesus came to earth to start a revolution, he did so by gathering a small band of **ordinary men.**

OVERVIEW

These men had their own unique backgrounds, diverse occupations, and individual personalities. It was alongside one another that Jesus would orchestrate learning environments that would change them into the most powerful transformative community in the history of the world.

Together, these men went from being self-centered individuals to united powerhouses that forever changed the course of history. Jesus didn't just teach them wonderful truths. He modeled, coached, and empowered them on what it took to make those truths become a living reality in the challenging world in which they lived. Please hear this when we say, "Jesus is still forming and empowering communities today."

Our hope is that this 5-session small group experience is the beginning of a journey that transforms your group into this type of community.

Here are the basic elements we have prepared for you:

5 SHORT FILMS

We believe in the power of story. The 5 films connected with Series 1 are stories of real people facing real life challenges.

5-PART DISCUSSION GUIDE

We believe in the power of community. This guide will help facilitate small group interaction in a way that creates connection around things that matter.

5-PART PERSONAL STUDY AND SCRIPTURE REFLECTION

We believe in the power of personal study and reflection. This gives the opportunity, between group meetings, to move the ideas from the film and discussion into deeper understanding and growth.

GROUP DYNAMICS

COMBINED WITH THE FILMS, THE 5-SESSION GROUP DISCUSSION IS DESIGNED TO MAXIMIZE INTERACTION, CONNECTION AND MEANINGFUL CONVERSATIONS.

We've intentionally made this guide as straightforward as possible. Please know that each of these simple steps are specifically designed to help create maximum impact for you and your group. With that in mind, we encourage you to trust the process by following each step along with its suggested time frame.

CORE GROUP TIME CONSISTS OF:

1. Opening Prayer. Surrendering time and hearts to God's leading.

2. Check In. Discussing past week's issues, progress, and challenges.

3. Watch Film. Viewing together a 10- to 14-minute real-life story.

4. Discussion. Sharing personal impressions and thoughts about the film.

5. Next Steps. Discussing a measurable step that can be taken this coming week.

6. Personal Study Preview. Brief look at this week's personal study.

7. Closing Prayer. Asking for God's guidance and strength for the week ahead.

Each meeting together will serve as an opportunity to connect with each other, get real, build trust, and consider the important issues in the lives of everyone in your group.

IDEAL GROUP SIZE & TIME FRAME

An ideal small group size is 5–7. If the group is too small and somebody does not come or drops out, you can lose the collective perspective and encouragement a group can bring. If it is too large, you lose the opportunity for everyone to fully participate and build trust. If your group is larger, you can break into smaller groups for the discussion time. If you are meeting as a large group, we strongly encourage you keep the smaller groups together throughout your 5 sessions.

An ideal time frame for your group is 90 minutes. Of course, if your group decides, you can meet for longer or shorter periods. We recommend not meeting for less than 60 minutes. The suggested meeting agenda we have provided is based on the 90-minute time frame. If you meet longer or shorter, adjust accordingly.

Note that our language throughout is "each week." We find a lot of groups meet every other week. This can work great as well. For relational continuity we do not recommend meeting once a month.

GROUP FACILITATOR

We have consistently seen the #1 common denominator for most effective small groups is having one individual who is motivated to "owning" the group's formation, logistics, and reminders for the full 5 weeks. This will go a long way in seeing the group stay consistent and finish strong. Many times, that same guy guides the group through the discussion, but that is not always the case. The main responsibilities for an effective group facilitator are:

- Recruits men to join him in a 5-session small-group experience together.
- Makes sure everyone gets a study guide.
- Makes sure the meeting place and film watching portion are good to go.
- Communicates meeting time reminders and encouragement between gatherings.

MEETING LOGISTICS

The group dynamic is designed around watching a short film together each time you meet. This will require having the means to play the films and access to a proper screen and sound system. In choosing the meeting place, the fewer distractions you have, the greater the chance for open discussion. Some churches host larger gatherings of men who sit around individual tables. They all watch the film together and participate in all the discussion time at their tables. If you do this, we encourage you to keep the same guys at each table each week in order to build trust.

FIRST SESSION ORIENTATION

Please be sure that your group goes over the Sharing and Group Guidelines in the first session and has a chance to ask any clarification questions. Have the group agree to commit to these Guidelines. They are simple yet designed to enhance your experience together.

OVERVIEW

Here is how everything fits together for this series.

- Each meeting you will go through the Group Discussion Guide, watch a film, and discuss personal relevance and application.
- In between each session, you will go through the Personal Study and Scripture Reflection to process the major theme of that film and think more deeply on supporting Scriptures.
- At the next meeting you will have an opportunity to discuss what you discovered, worked through, and what stood out to you during your Personal Study and Scripture Reflection time.

We encourage your group to consider at least one "off the script" meeting (i.e., BBQ, movie, sporting event, games, cards, etc.). We lay these out more fully at coreunites.com/whatsnext.

In the first session together, please read out loud these guidelines for everyone to have an opportunity to discuss and agree to.

GROUP DISCUSSION GUIDELINES

We believe that if you can stay within the riverbanks of these four guidelines, you will maximize a positive small experience for everyone.

1. Personalize, Not Sermonize. What does the specific issue being discussed mean for my life, my concerns, my dreams versus the need to give additional insights to others? The courage to speak from personal transparency contributes significantly to everyone in your group. Speak more from the "I", "my", "me" and NOT the "you" and "we" position. This can be difficult for those of us who are teachers or those who wish to be seen as insightful.

2. Be Brief. Be thoughtful not to dominate discussion time. Think in terms of 1-2 minutes each time you share. If you know you are someone who loves to share, discipline yourself to actively listen. If you have something that needs more time to unpack, make a request to discuss it later. Being brief can be difficult for those of us who externally process versus those who internalize thoughts before speaking.

3. Encourage, Not Fix. We honor courageous authenticity. We discourage group counsel or correction. We need to take responsibility for our own actions, results, and experiences. This can be difficult for those of us who are counselors or "fixers."

4. Maintain Confidentiality. Keep everything shared confidential. Do not repeat it to ANYONE outside your CORE group, including spouses or close friends. This can be difficult for those of us who don't highly value what it means to be a trusted confidante.

SMALL GROUP COURTESTY "101s"

- If you are going to be late or absent, call someone in your group to inform them.
- No cellphone use during the meeting, unless permission is asked at the beginning of the meeting.
- Don't leave the group permanently without speaking to your group about it.

There are **5 films** that go along with *CORE for Men: Redeemed.* These are a central component to the small-group experience.

ADDITIONAL SMALL GROUP BEST PRACTICES

Here are some additional small group dynamic insights that will be beneficial for your CORE group to be aware of:

- The purpose of a CORE group is to encourage us to think and discuss from a personal heart perspective. When the film ends, go directly into the first discussion question, "What part of _____ story or sharing stuck out to you?"

- The CORE discussion time is a simple invitation to be real. No posturing required. "Being real" can mean different things to different people. So, be respectful of each other and embrace what "being real" means for them. That includes not making anyone feel like they have to share something personal. When everyone in a group feels like they can relax and be themselves, it's surprising how God will help open up the group's interaction over time.

- Interrupt any tendency you feel to judge another. We get enough of that already.

- Avoid being an "advice giver." If someone in the group wants input or feedback, let them ask for it. If you have input you want to offer, ask permission to give it. Feel free to not grant permission to someone to give input if you are not ready to hear it from them.

- Do not shut down someone who may choose to use strong language or express raw emotion in describing their perspective and experience (i.e., swearing, raising voice, etc.).

- Be respectful of the time frames included in the meeting agenda for each week. As briefly discussed earlier in our Group Guidelines, a common problem is the tendency of one guy to dominate the group time. If someone is going over on time, after the meeting, respectfully remind them of the guidelines. If they persist, kindly remind them during the group time out of respect for the rest of the group.

- There will be some very good and open conversations in the "Check In" and "Discussion" time. Make sure you leave yourselves a little room for the "Next Steps," "Personal Study Preview," and "Closing Prayer" time.
- The current culture is high on talking but slow on doing. When you purposefully give time to ask, "What specific step am I going to take this week?" it can move your group into new levels of discovery and breakthrough. This also gives everyone something specific to pray for one another during the week.
- In your first time together, write down everyone's name in this guide and during the week, take a moment to pray for each guy by name. It doesn't have to be a long prayer. Watch what happens to your own heart toward the guys in your group when you do this. It's pretty awesome to see how your heart changes toward the group.
- When you discuss how your previous week's "Next Steps" and "Personal Study" went, this is a "no shame zone." Growth and new habits take time. Empathy, encouragement, and patience go a long way toward building the kind of environment that will surface root issues and facilitate breakthrough.
- Pay attention to the men in your group. If it seems like there might be a guy who would have an easier time opening up "one on one," look for an opportunity to grab a coffee or a bite to eat. These moments can be great for some guys.
- Finally, a great CORE group meeting, which takes time to evolve, has an ease and a flow to it. It is not a rigidly enforced agenda, but it is important to follow the established guidelines that allow enough time for each of the group elements.

LET'S GO!

SESSION

CALLED

MARIANO RIVERA

GROUP DISCUSSION GUIDE (90 MINUTES)

OPENING PRAYER
Surrender your time and heart to God's leading.

CHECK IN (15 MINUTES—1–2 MINUTES PER PERSON)

1. Share your name.

2. Main reasons for wanting to be in the group.

3. One thing you would like to get from participating in the group.

TOGETHER READ THE GUIDELINES ON PAGE 9. (15 MINUTES)
These are simple yet designed to enhance your group experience.

1. Does everyone in the group understand them?

2. Are there any clarification questions regarding any of the guidelines?

3. Can we commit to these as a group?

Note: Many of you are seeing this study guide for the first time. There is some foundational information in the Overview and Group Dynamics section that would be well worth reading before you meet again.

WATCH FILM (11 MINUTES)
Called—Mariano Rivera

GROUP DISCUSSION (35 MINUTES)
Be mindful of the need for everyone to have the opportunity to talk. Take 1–2 minutes each time you share.

1. Which part of Mariano's story did you connect with?

2. Mariano said that his pitch's new movement was not something he deserved or was asking for but was a gift that gave him a platform to honor God. Have you ever thought that way about a strength or ability in your life? Explain.

NEXT STEPS (10 MINUTES)

In light of today's discussion, what is one step you can take in your life or in your relationships this week? Something specific. Something measurable. Something the group can pray for during the week.

THE PURPOSE OF THE PERSONAL STUDY AND SCRIPTURE REFLECTION—READ OUT LOUD (2 MINUTES)

The Personal Study and Scripture Reflection section in this guide is included in each of the sessions. Taking time each week to do them can be one of the most important things you choose to do over these next 5 weeks. It is the difference between randomly throwing seed on the ground versus planting it deeply. Setting aside time for personal study and prayerful reflection is a new rhythm for many. Committing to this, along with showing up every week with your group, will strengthen your ability to drop old thoughts and habits and take on new ways to think and live.

PERSONAL STUDY EXCERPT—READ OUT LOUD (2 MINUTES)

God made Mariano in His own image, and God led him to a particular place, with a particular talent, to show God's character to a particular people. He began to see with more and more clarity, that God was weaving His grand story within the particulars of his own personal story. Mariano said, "It was something that the Lord gave me to give me a platform to talk about Him. Not because I was asking. Not because I deserved it. But He wanted to use that to glorify His name." God has a purpose for His people. It's such a wild thought, isn't it? The God of the universe has chosen to collaborate with ordinary, everyday, imperfect people. He doesn't do this because He's been forced to and it's definitely not because He needs to, but solely because He wants to.

CLOSING PRAYER

Ask for God's guidance and strength for the week ahead.

CORE GROUP NOTES

⊛ PERSONAL STUDY

Given Mariano's status as the greatest relief pitcher in the history of baseball, it might at first be hard to relate to how his journey began. It started with him having virtually no awareness of a particular calling or specific purpose. Calling and purpose were probably the furthest things from his mind. Yet, regardless of what Mariano was or was not aware of, it is clear from his story that God had a calling and purpose for his life.

In the same way, God has a specific calling and purpose for you. Look at what He says to you in His Word:

You did not choose me, but I chose you and appointed you so that you might go and bear fruit—fruit that will last—and so that whatever you ask in my name the Father will give you. **John 15:16 (NIV)**

God chose the lowly things of this world and the despised things—and the things that are not—to nullify the things that are, so that no one may boast before him. **1 Corinthians 1:28–29 (NIV)**

God has a purpose for His people. It's such a wild thought, isn't it? The God of the universe has chosen to collaborate with ordinary, everyday, imperfect people. He doesn't do this because He's been forced to and it's definitely not because He needs to, but solely because He wants to.

God made you in His image. **Genesis 1:26 (ESV)** clearly states our original purpose and calling:

Then God said, "Let us make man in our image, after our likeness. And let them have dominion over the fish of the sea and over the birds of the heavens and over the livestock and over all the earth and over every creeping thing that creeps on the earth."

This means that the all-encompassing aim of your life is to reflect God to others. That looks unique for each one of us. We all have different jobs, different families, live in different homes, have different backgrounds, and so on. But there are some constants for everyone—such as reflecting God's love, His goodness, His compassion, His forgiveness, just to name a few. All of us are called to reflect God to specific people in certain places and times.

God calls you and gives gifts to you in order to fulfill that calling. He has made you in His image. He chose you. He loves you. And you did absolutely nothing to earn it. That is the good news of God's grace! No pressure to earn it, perform for it, or try to achieve it. God freely offers it. He paid the price in full. It is a free gift (Romans 5:15; 6:23).

Consider the status of Mariano's life when God called him. It was well before Mariano had accomplished any level of success in his life. God did not choose him because he was successful—because at that time he wasn't. God chose him because God loved him, and it was for God's purposes. God is on the move and He's chosen to use ordinary people to partner with Him and His purposes. Just as He invited Mariano to collaborate with Him, He is inviting us to do the same.

When you get a glimpse of the life of Mariano Rivera, you see the uniqueness of God's calling. We're talking about the best closer in major league history. When he stepped on the mound in the ninth inning, he dominated unlike anyone before or after him. But his story is much more than being a great pitcher. It's a love story of God pursuing him, changing him, and collaborating with him.

> GOD MADE MARIANO IN HIS OWN IMAGE, AND GOD LED HIM TO A PARTICULAR PLACE, WITH A PARTICULAR TALENT, TO SHOW GOD'S CHARACTER TO A PARTICULAR PEOPLE.

Even before Mariano committed his life to Christ, he became aware that God was trying to get his and his wife's attention. God had been using each of Mariano's circumstances to soften his heart and to open his eyes. One day, he heard a pastor give an invitation to become a follower of Jesus. It was then, on that day, that he confessed Jesus as his Lord and made Him his Savior.

THE TWO MOST
IMPORTANT DAYS
IN YOUR LIFE
ARE THE DAY YOU
WERE BORN AND
THE DAY YOU
FOUND OUT WHY.

Mark Twain

If you openly declare that Jesus is Lord and believe in your heart that God raised him from the dead, you will be saved. For it is by believing in your heart that you are made right with God, and it is by openly declaring your faith that you are saved. **Romans 10:9–10 (NLT)**

Mariano said, "That was the moment that I said, 'I surrender. I can't do this thing anymore.' That moment was something special . . . I said to God, whatever you want us to do, we are here."

He began to see with more and more clarity, that God was weaving His grand story within the particulars of his own human story.

Mariano started noticing God's work in very specific things, including baseball. For example, when Mariano threw the ball—just as he always had—it started moving toward the catcher in ways that he had never experienced before. Batters were rarely able to get a hit off his pitches, and Mariano knew that God had given him this particular ability for a purpose.

Mariano said, "It was something that the Lord gave me to give me a platform to talk about Him. Not because I was asking. Not because I deserved it. But He wanted to use that to glorify his name."

This is indeed a gift—God giving something that was not earned or expected. A gift is not based upon accomplishments, dedication, hard work, talent, or effort. A gift is something that the Giver has decided to impart simply because He wants to and loves to.

How many gifts from God go unnoticed or unappreciated for what they are? It is so easy to experience blessings in our relationships and careers without seeing them for what they really are. They are all opportunities to experience the graciousness of God in our lives and to use them to honor Him.

We use the gifts that God has given us in one of two ways: to honor God, or to honor ourselves. Oftentimes we can start believing that we are the ones who are responsible for these gifts in our lives. But Mariano shares with us that it's through the difficult times of life that we are reminded of how powerless we really are—and how powerful God is. It is when things don't turn out the way we want them, when we go through times of failure and unmet expectations, that we are given the gift of facing our own inabilities.

Here is a secret worth discovering: when we come face to face with inabilities and weaknesses and learn how to surrender those to the King of Grace, there exists freedom and joy. It is as simple as praying, "God, I can't do this, I can't face this, but I ask You to help me take the first steps to let You do through me what I'm struggling with on my own."

This is what Paul is encouraging the Corinthians with the counterintuitive secret God revealed to him.

But he said to me, "My grace is sufficient for you, for my power is made perfect in weakness." Therefore I will boast all the more gladly about my weaknesses, so that Christ's power may rest on me.
2 Corinthians 12:9 (NIV)

Are you willing to see hardships that way? Ask yourself this CRUCIAL question:

When I go through the fire of life's challenges, am I willing to become less dependent on myself and more dependent on God?

We must believe that we can face our own weakness because God is always seeking to draw our hearts closer to Him—and few things in the world can draw us nearer to God than difficulties. He is always faithful to grant us the grace and courage necessary to stand firm during these times. When we come out of that fire, we will be stronger and more faithful than when we went into it.

One of the ways we are able to persevere with hope is by the gift of community. Mariano said that Willie Alfonso was a powerful influence during the hardest seasons of his life. Willie was a person who was always there for Mariano. He was one of God's provisions for Mariano to recognize that life is not meant to be figured out on one's own.

AS YOU THINK ABOUT THOSE IN YOUR CORE GROUP:

- Trust that God has provided them for you to encourage and strengthen your faith.

- Trust that God has provided you for them to encourage and strengthen their faith.

God has gathered each of you together to be a support for one another through the fires.

Think about the challenges you currently face in your life: work, family, children, spouse, and all the other facets of your life.

Let this 5-week CORE journey be an opportunity to be as real as possible with one another, to come alongside one another and to experience significant breakthroughs together.

PERSONAL STUDY NOTES

SCRIPTURE REFLECTION

PERSONAL STUDY QUESTIONS

Some things become clearer when you take the time to actually write down your thoughts. Though it is not a familiar practice for many, consider taking a few minutes with each of these 4 questions:

1. What was one thing that struck me most from my Personal Study reading?

2. What is one area of my life where I could really use a breakthrough?

3. What, if any, fears do I have that create obstacles to seeing God work in and through me?

4. Have I addressed my "Next Steps" that I shared with my CORE group? If not, what is keeping me from addressing it?

SCRIPTURE REFLECTION PRACTICE

We encourage you to consider the following Scripture passage over the course of this week in a prayerfully contemplative way. This simple process will help you engage not only your mind but also your heart. Consider focusing this week on the same Scripture below (Ephesians 2:4-10) each day, using these principles:

- Be alert for a phrase or word that catches your attention. This could be in the form of a question on what it means or a new insight.

- Once during the week, read the verse aloud slowly.

- Once during the week, as you read the verses, pause along the way to use it to spark specific prayers to God.

- Finally, after reading the verses, pause to be thankful that, "it is God who works in you, both to will and to work for his good pleasure." **Philippians 2:13 (ESV)**

SCRIPTURE REFLECTION FOR SESSION 1:
EPHESIANS 2:4–10 (NIV)

But God, being rich in mercy, because of the great love with which he loved us, even when we were dead in our trespasses, made us alive together with Christ—by grace you have been saved— and raised us up with him and seated us with him in the heavenly places in Christ Jesus, so that in the coming ages he might show the immeasurable riches of his grace in kindness toward us in Christ Jesus.

For by grace you have been saved through faith. And this is not your own doing; it is the gift of God, not a result of works, so that no one may boast. For we are his workmanship, created in Christ Jesus for good works, which God prepared beforehand, that we should walk in them.

SCRIPTURE REFLECTION NOTES

REDEMPTION

KYLE OXFORD

GROUP DISCUSSION GUIDE 90 MINUTES

OPENING PRAYER

Surrender your time and heart to God's leading.

CHECK IN (20 MINUTES—2–3 MINUTES PER PERSON)

1. How has your week gone? Family? Work?

2. What kind of progress or challenges did you have with your "Next Steps" from last sesssion?

3. How was your Personal Study and Scripture Reflection time this week? What is resonating? What is not working?

WATCH FILM (10 MINUTES)

Redemption—Kyle Oxford

GROUP DISCUSSION (45 MINUTES)

1. Which part of Kyle's story did you connect with?

2. Where have you seen God redeem losses in your life or those around you? Explain.

NEXT STEPS (10 MINUTES)

Be mindful of the need for everyone to have an opportunity to talk. Take 2–3 minutes each. Take notes and pray for each other's "Next Steps" during the week. As always, keep everything confidential.

In light of today's discussion, what is one step you can take in your life or in your relationships this week? Something specific. Something measurable. Something the group can pray for during the week.

PERSONAL STUDY EXCERPT—READ OUT LOUD (5 MINUTES)

Kyle's story is a striking reminder of how God redeems losses, even when those losses are life altering and life defining. Through all the difficulty, Kyle came to understand a powerful truth when he shares, "Just facing myself and facing God and saying, 'I need you' was tough. I felt so unworthy of anything . . . even a response. But He was faithful and showed up and He met me where I was." You can trust Him, and you can turn to Him even in the darkest of seasons. Why? Because Jesus understands and paid the ultimate price to allow you bold access to God's mercy and grace.

CLOSING PRAYER

Ask for God's guidance and strength during the week ahead.

CORE GROUP NOTES

👁 PERSONAL STUDY

Knowing that you're made in the image of God and that God invites you to reflect Him to others is a captivating thought. It puts wind in your sails like nothing or nobody else could.

There is a calling, but there is also an assault.

The Scriptures remind us that forces are actively seeking to keep us from experiencing our intended design and purpose. It's often difficult for many to understand, but there is a spiritual adversary who tries to rob you of hope, faithfulness, and obedience.

1 Peter 5:8 (ESV) tells us to, *"Be sober-minded; be watchful. Your adversary the devil prowls around like a roaring lion, seeking someone to devour."* The reality of this assault is evident in Kyle's story. His dream of marriage and family turned into a nightmare of rejection and emasculation. Kyle's openness allows us to see how the enemy can use people and circumstances to wound us.

But even in the face of hurt, pain, and disappointment, God's faithfulness is evident in the way He redeems even the darkest seasons of life.

We all have dark seasons of life, don't we? Maybe you can remember the heaviness of deep sorrow or helplessness. Maybe you are in that season right now.

In the same way that each of our specific callings look different, the attacks each of us experience from the enemy look different.

For some, it's the experience of sudden, life-altering moments that cause deep wounds. For others, the attack is slow and rigorous, spread out over a much longer period of time.

In the boxing ring, sometimes a fighter is knocked out by a quick and powerful blow to the head. Often times, it's the round after round of blows to the body that weakens and drops the defenses. Ultimately, this constant attack is what sets up the blow that ends it.

Whether we want to admit it or not, we are in a war—a war over the domain of our affections and decisions. The question is not really whether are *in* a war but whether are we *at* war. So, a critical issue for us to consider is how we are going to face and win the battles ahead.

God tells us in **Romans 8:28 (NASB)** that He,*"causes all things to work together for good to those who love God, to those who are called according to His purpose."*

But when you're in the middle of these grueling and despairing seasons, it often doesn't feel that way. It can feel like the solutions are far away, if they exist at all.

Kyle's story is a striking reminder of how God redeems losses, even when those losses are life altering and life defining. As you read them below, consider the reflective questions in bold fonts. In your Personal Study notes section, write what comes to mind as you consider those questions.

"When I was younger, I had dreams... like dreams of being a father and being a husband and being a good husband. When our marriage dissolved, it forced me to forget about those dreams. And that began the downward spiral for me."

What expectations and/or dreams have you had that were shattered?

"After that I was in a season of wandering. I remember just feeling like God didn't care about me or my circumstances. I was in a period of rejecting Him. I remember one day just making my mind up that I didn't care what He thought. I didn't care if He existed. I was going to do my own thing because surely it wouldn't or couldn't hurt any more than I already hurt."

THE MEANING OF REDEMPTION IS THAT WE DO NOT HAVE TO BE OUR HISTORY.

Flannery O'Connor

Have you ever rebelled against God because of being hurt or disappointed?

"I had the first real conversation that I ever had with God that morning. I said I don't know who you are, I believe that you're there, but I need you to help me, and rescue me out of this. I just laid down on the trail and cried out to God. I wasn't asking for a favor. I wasn't asking for my life to be blessed. I wasn't asking for anything really but for him to have mercy on me."

Kyle cried out to God. He held nothing back and was as real with God as he knew how to be. Where in your life do you need to get entirely real with God and have this kind of conversation?

"Just facing myself and facing God and saying, 'I need you' was tough. I felt so unworthy of anything . . . even a response. But He was faithful and showed up, and He met me where I was."

God responds when we are brutally honest and vulnerable with Him. David's example in the Psalms of raw authenticity is a great example of this.

"After I had cried out to God and was reconciled to him, some of the dreams I'd had as a kid started coming back to me, and the dreams that I had on my wedding day years before were coming back. I realized that I needed to start moving in the direction of the dreams that God had put before me. And Megan is somebody who was my ideal. She was number one in terms of the kind of woman that I wanted to be with."

What does it tell you about God's character that He loves to surprise us with gifts that are undeserved?

"I don't believe that God's plan was for me to get divorced or for Megan's husband to die and leave behind a widow with two kids. But I do believe that God is really good at taking the broken pieces and making something beautiful out of them. The life that I have now is beyond what I had ever imagined or dreamed of, and I'm really excited about the future that I have with Megan and with our kids. I'm excited to see what God does next."

Have you ever experienced a time where God took something broken and turned it into something beautiful?

"All of our stories look different on the outside, but at their core they are truly the same. We have our own circumstances, our own day-to-day realities, but just like everyone, we know the feeling of struggle."

The thief does not come except to steal, and to kill, and to destroy. I have come that they may have life, and that they may have it more abundantly. **John 10:10 (NKJV)**

You have an adversary. Along the course of your life, you're going to take some big hits. But God is more powerful, and He redeems losses. You can trust Him, and you can turn to Him even in the darkest of seasons. Why? Because Jesus understands and paid the ultimate price to allow you bold access to God's mercy and grace.

This High Priest of ours understands our weaknesses, for he faced all of the same testings we do, yet he did not sin. So let us come boldly to the throne of our gracious God. There we will receive his mercy, and we will find grace to help us when we need it most. **Hebrews 4:15–16 (NLT)**

PERSONAL STUDY NOTES

SCRIPTURE REFLECTION

PERSONAL STUDY QUESTIONS

1. What dreams have you given up on that you desire God to restore?

2. Is there an area of "brokenness" in your life that you could wait expectantly for God to redeem into something beautiful?

3. Have I addressed my action step that I shared with my CORE Group? If not, what is keeping me from stepping out and addressing it? What's my next step?

SCRIPTURE REFLECTION PRACTICE

We encourage you to consider the following Scripture passage over the course of this week in a prayerfully contemplative way. This simple process will help you engage not only your mind but also your heart. Consider focusing this week on the same Scripture below (1 Peter 5:6–11) each day, using these principles:

- Be alert for a phrase or word that catches your attention. This could be in the form of a question on what it means or a new insight.
- Once during the week, read the verse aloud slowly.
- Once during the week, as you read the verses, pause along the way to use it to spark specific prayers to God.
- Finally, after reading the verses, pause to be thankful that *"it is God who works in you, both to will and to work for his good pleasure."* **Philippians 2:13 (ESV)**

SCRIPTURE REFLECTION FOR SESSION 2: 1 PETER 5:6–11 (NIV)

Humble yourselves, therefore, under the mighty hand of God so that at the proper time he may exalt you, casting all your anxieties on him, because he cares for you.

Be sober-minded; be watchful. Your adversary the devil prowls around like a roaring lion, seeking someone to devour. Resist him, firm in your faith, knowing that the same kinds of suffering are being experienced by your brotherhood throughout the world.

And after you have suffered a little while, the God of all grace, who has called you to his eternal glory in Christ, will himself restore, confirm, strengthen, and establish you. To him be the dominion forever and ever. Amen.

SCRIPTURE REFLECTION NOTES

SONS

TOMMY GREEN

GROUP DISCUSSION GUIDE 90 MINUTES

OPENING PRAYER
Surrender your time and heart to God's leading.

CHECK IN (20 MINUTES)
Be mindful that you are not taking more time to talk than the others in the group.

1. How has your week gone? Family? Work?

2. What kind of progress or challenges did you have with your "Next Step" from last session?

3. How was your Personal Study and Scripture Reflection time this week? What is resonating? What is not working?

No judgment zone. Remember that we are here to listen. Consider, how can I understand and encourage?

WATCH FILM (13 MINUTES)
Sons—Tommy Green

GROUP DISCUSSION (45 MINUTES)

1. What part of Tommy's story did you connect with?

2. How do you think your father would answer your question, "How do you feel about me?"

3. Have you ever felt the necessity to pursue or reconcile with someone when you knew there was little chance for reciprocation? What happened when you did or did not follow through with it?

NEXT STEPS (10 MINUTES)

In light of today's discussion, what is one step you can take in your life or in your relationships this week? Something specific. Something measurable. Something the group can pray for during the week.

Be mindful of the need for everyone to have an opportunity to talk. Take 2–3 minutes each. Take notes and pray for each other's action steps during the week. As always, keep everything confidential.

PERSONAL STUDY EXCERPT—READ OUT LOUD (2 MINUTES)
Tommy has taken the abandonment and rage that he felt and has seen God redeem it. Instead of being ruled by them, these deep emotions have become an offering of thanks to God for the new identity He has given us all . . . to be HIS CHILDREN. Our choice is to rage against the unfairness of the world we were born into or to embrace the path of sonship that God has freely offered us.

CLOSING PRAYER
Ask for God's guidance and strength during the week ahead.

CORE GROUP NOTES

🔒 PERSONAL STUDY

Tommy Green's story is intense and sobering.

It's the story of one man's struggle with the ongoing impact of a father's anger and abuse. It is about a man who desired to become free from his rage and inner doubts, and ultimately become an agent of healing in his culture.

What is Tommy's vision for himself and the young people who listen to his music? He tells us, "Hopefully, I've become a father in an orphaned culture."

Tommy is in the process of transforming the pain of his father's abuse into a passion for being a father to a fatherless generation. He has sought and found an outlet to stay real and still have that authenticity be a form of worship instead of destruction.

> No matter the circumstance, you can trust in your Heavenly Father's character. He truly is always trustworthy.

In the film, Tommy said:

"I had fury as a son, and I had deep loss and rejection with nowhere to put it."

"Fire . . . if you put it in the right thing it can warm the house, right? If you just let it go, it'll burn the house down. So, I felt like this (his music) can be like my fire. I can put all that I'm feeling in this thing and it can go somewhere. It gave my absolute rage and abandonment toward my father, toward my stepfather, toward this whole planet, toward God . . .

I could put all of it in context. And I knew other people felt like me. It gave my pain a voice in that."

"When I met Jesus for real, I just wanted to create worship that made sense to me [and] wouldn't alienate my culture, but at the same time would build a bridge so that eventually people could worship together."

"We did a show in Southern California. I remember it was with a whole bunch of kids and I remember it was in San Bernardino on Father's Day. There were like 5,000 people. And I remember going, 'Yeah, there's 5,000 dudes here at this show not with their dads.' So, we are ministering to a gaping wound in a generation . . . that cycle of fatherlessness . . . that hunger . . . that void that isn't quite met is the root of all sorts of dysfunction and sorrow and pain."

Tommy has taken the abandonment and rage that he felt and has seen God redeem it. Instead of being ruled by them, these deep emotions have become an offering of thanks to God for the new identity He has given us all...to be HIS CHILDREN. Our choice is to rage against the unfairness of the world we were born into or to embrace the path of sonship that God has freely offered us.

Some of these verses were addressed earlier, but their brilliance is worth repeating:

For all who are led by the Spirit of God are sons of God. For you did not receive the spirit of slavery to fall back into fear, but you have received the Spirit of adoption as sons, by whom we cry, "Abba! Father!" The Spirit himself bears witness with our spirit that we are children of God, and if children, then heirs—heirs of God and fellow heirs with Christ, provided we suffer with him in order that we may also be glorified with him. **Romans 8:14–17 (ESV)**

The phrase "Abba Father" is interesting. *Abba* is an Aramaic word most closely related to the word *daddy* today. Jesus opened the path for us to have a deeply intimate relationship with God, our Father.

But He is not some distant authority figure that is inaccessible to us. He is our Daddy. He desires intimacy with us. He wants to hold us close to His heart and shower us with His love.

Fatherlessness is an ongoing, catastrophic crisis in our culture today. The only sure solution for this is to embrace God as our "Abba father"—our Daddy. To embrace His love, grace, and mercy toward us. He tells us He will never leave us or forsake us **(Hebrews 13:5)**.

As humans, we are weak and fall short. As the God of the universe, He is strong and reliable. Even when it looks like nothing is working, He is still there.

How was your relationship with your father? Even if you never met him (which would also impact you). You might have the closest of relationships with your father, or you might only know him by his absence. The impact of your father is significant, for better or for worse.

Gary Stanley said, "Fathers interpret life for their children—give life structure and meaning. They do so whether they mean to or not. It either becomes the foundation on which we build a life, or the rubble we dig out from under."

No father is perfect. Most are far from perfect. How you relate to your father's imperfections influences much of your life. Tommy Green eventually saw that fully embracing the love extended to him by His heavenly Father was the key to transforming his way of relating to the rejection of his earthly father. Tommy's trust in the true Fatherhood of God has moved him from rage to redemption.

If Christ is your Savior, then God is your Father. He invites you into an intimate relationship with Him. He will never leave you or forsake you. He is good, even in the worst of times. No matter the circumstance, you can trust in your heavenly Father's character. As we addressed in an earlier film, He truly is always trustworthy to take our broken things and make something beautiful out of them. Tommy's life illustrates this.

Leaning into this reality and allowing it to heal you from the wounds of your past is the key to not paying the rage forward. It can heal your fury while moving you toward forgiveness, love, joy, peace, forbearance, kindness, goodness, faithfulness, gentleness, and self-control **(Galatians 5:22)**.

This takes time. It takes obedience. It takes a commitment to grow and change. And, most of all, it takes trusting God that He is who He says He is, and He will do what He says He will do.

It's worth the risk. Your legacy hangs in the balance before you.

PERSONAL STUDY NOTES

SCRIPTURE REFLECTION

 **PERSONAL STUDY QUESTIONS**

1. What was missing for you in your relationship with your father? Even if you have or had a great relationship with your dad, no father is perfect. What was missing for you?

2. How do you think it might influence your relationship with God as your Father?

3. Have I addressed my "Next Steps" that I shared with my CORE group? If not, what is keeping me from stepping out and addressing it? What's my next step?

SCRIPTURE REFLECTION PRACTICE

We encourage you to consider the following Scripture passage over the course of this week in a prayerfully contemplative way. This simple process will help you engage not only your mind but also your heart. Consider focusing this week on the same Scripture below (Romans 8:12–17) each day, using these principles:

- Be alert for a phrase or word that catches your attention. This could be in the form of a question on what it means or a new insight.
- Once during the week, read the verse aloud slowly.
- Once during the week, as you read the verses, pause along the way to use it to spark specific prayers to God.
- Finally, after reading the verses, pause to be thankful that, "it is God who works in you, both to will and to work for his good pleasure." **Philippians 2:13 (ESV)**

SCRIPTURE REFLECTION FOR SESSION 3: ROMANS 8:12–17 (ESV)

So then, brothers, we are debtors, not to the flesh, to live according to the flesh. For if you live according to the flesh you will die, but if by the Spirit you put to death the deeds of the body, you will live.

For all who are led by the Spirit of God are sons of God. For you did not receive the spirit of slavery to fall back into fear, but you have received the Spirit of adoption as sons, by whom we cry, "Abba! Father!"

The Spirit himself bears witness with our spirit that we are children of God, and if children, then heirs—heirs of God and fellow heirs with Christ, provided we suffer with him in order that we may also be glorified with him.

SCRIPTURE REFLECTION NOTES

SESSION

4

RESTORATION

SHARON & ROBERT IRVING

GROUP DISCUSSION GUIDE 90 MINUTES

OPENING PRAYER

Surrender your time and heart to God's leading.

CHECK IN (20 MINUTES)

Be mindful that you are not taking more time to talk than the others in the group

1. How has your week gone? Family? Work?

2. What kind of progress or challenges did you have with your "Next Step" from last session?

3. How was your Personal Study and Scripture Reflection time this week? What is resonating? What is not working?

Check In time is high on encouragement and low on "accountability."

WATCH FILM (14 MINUTES)

Restoration—Sharon & Robert Irving

GROUP DISCUSSION (40 MINUTES)

This is an opportunity to share from a personal perspective. How is this impacting *me*? Not a time to share general insights.

1. Which part of Sharon and Robert's story did you connect with?

2. Which of your relationships might need to be reconciled? What do you desire for those relationships?

NEXT STEPS (10 MINUTES)

Be mindful of the need for everyone to have an opportunity to talk. Take 2–3 minutes each. Take notes and pray for each other's action steps during the week. As always, keep everything confidential.

In light of today's discussion, what is one step you can take in your life or in your relationships this week? Something specific. Something measurable. Something the group can pray for during the week.

PERSONAL STUDY EXCERPT—READ OUT LOUD (5 MINUTES)

Reconciliation creates an avenue for working through the baggage of broken relationships and being at peace with one another. If you don't resolve to work toward reconciliation, the baggage of the brokenness will bleed out onto others who you say you care about. Pastor Tim Keller challenges us to take the initiative. "In its most basic and simple form, this teaching is that Christians in community are to never give up on one another, never give up on a relationship, and never write off another believer. We must never tire of forgiving and repenting and seeking to repair our relationships with one another. In short, if any relationship has cooled off or has weakened in any way, it is always your move. It doesn't matter 'who started it': God always holds you responsible to reach out to repair a tattered relationship. A Christian is responsible to begin the process of reconciliation, regardless of how the distance or the alienation began."

CLOSING PRAYER

Ask for God's guidance and strength during the week ahead.

CORE GROUP NOTES

⚠ PERSONAL STUDY

The Irvings are in the midst of a real-life, real-time reconciliation. The transparency they show as they struggle to resolve their disappointments into deeper love and connection is inspiring.

Often, when the nature of a relationship is breaking down or is not what we desire, we tend to think, "It is what it is." It doesn't occur to us that there is a possibility of restarting the relationship into something deeper, more connected, and more fulfilling. It may seem like the current state of the relationship is out of your hands, and that helpless feeling often continues into adulthood.

But, guess what? God says we are given the *ministry of reconciliation*. First, we must personally reconcile with our heavenly Father, which in turn will naturally stir up seeking reconciliation with others. He is the God who sent His Son to reconcile us back into relationship with Him. We get to reflect Him to others by being Ambassadors—Ambassadors of The Reconciler. (**2 Corinthians 5:18–20**)

This applies most powerfully in reconciling lost relationships. To reconcile means to bring back together that which has been separated. Where better to start than in the key relationships of your life that are estranged?

An appropriate place to start is by giving some thought about each of your relationships. What is the status of your rapport with your mom or dad, your stepparents, your children, your spouse, your ex-spouse, coworker, boss, friends, or acquaintances? In those relationships, where do you regret dropping the ball or making a mess of things?

Robert Irving's commitment to his work and travel schedule had a significant impact on his family. Tragically, this is not an isolated story; it's a very common one. It happens all the time as our commitment to work and success can become a counterfeit god. We can find ourselves willing to be mediocre in the most important things, to pursue excellence in lesser things. We might start embracing this with good intentions (paying the bills, supporting the family, etc.) without having a clear awareness of the impact it's having on those we love.

What you have to offer others is far more valuable than a paycheck or material provision. Though we must do everything possible to provide for our families, our greatest contributions are in the things that aren't immediately visible. Let's be honest: meeting the demanding challenges of work can feel far more satisfying than the relational challenges a husband and father face.

When you go to the beach and start swimming in ocean waters, many times you'll notice something peculiar. After 5 or 10 minutes of dodging the waves, you'll drift without even being aware. When you look back at where your friends and family are sitting on the beach, you'll notice that the currents have carried you hundreds of feet from where you started. It's typically a very slow and subtle drift.

> We must be careful not to purposefully neglect what and whom we value the most. Our lack of relational and emotional investment is a series of justifiable circumstances that turn into a subtle but lifelong drift—a drift that carries us away from what matters most.

As you consider these relationships, keep this in mind: You might notice even the slightest of fractures that need to be addressed and reconciled.

Robert Irving started to address the hurt caused by his absence while Sharon was growing up. Here is what Sharon said about her father's attempts to reconcile more deeply with her.

"To hear him be vulnerable and see him be vulnerable gave me such a different level of respect for him. It definitely did something to my heart, seeing him open up about very hard, uncomfortable things. It was something that I think I needed to get to this next level. And for the next chapter of our relationship, it was like a page turned almost."

FORGIVENESS FLOUNDERS BECAUSE I EXCLUDE THE ENEMY FROM THE COMMUNITY OF HUMANS EVEN AS I EXCLUDE MYSELF FROM THE COMMUNITY OF SINNERS.

Miroslav Volf

The Scriptures speak vividly about the priority and impact of reconciliation. While considering your own relationships, let these passages challenge and encourage you.

Therefore, if you are offering your gift at the altar and there remember that your brother or sister has something against you, leave your gift there in front of the altar. First go and be reconciled to them; then come and offer your gift. **Matthew 5:23–24 (NIV)**

If your brother sins against you, go and tell him his fault, between you and him alone. If he listens to you, you have gained your brother. **Matthew 18:15–16 (ESV)**

The Bible describes the healthiest of relationships as "iron sharpening iron." It's a way of consistently seeking out reconciliation with one another. It requires courage, humility, and forgiveness. It requires that you be okay with being seen as weak and not being right all the time. It means that you actively seek to work through the breakdown that has occurred with the other person. It also requires being vulnerable enough to state what your offense is, if you feel wronged by another. And you not only state it, you then engage a conversation about how to reconcile through it.

Reconciliation creates an avenue for working through the baggage of broken relationships and being at peace with one another. If you don't resolve to work toward reconciliation, the baggage of the brokenness will bleed out on others that you say you care about. Pastor Tim Keller challenges us to take the initiative. "In its most basic and simple form, this teaching is that Christians in community are to never give up on one another, never give up on a relationship, and never write off another believer. We must never tire of forgiving and repenting and seeking to repair our relationships with one another. In short, if any relationship has cooled off or has weakened in any way, it is always your move. It doesn't matter 'who started it': God always holds you responsible to reach out to repair a tattered relationship. A Christian is responsible to begin the process of reconciliation, regardless of how the distance or the alienation began."

Jesus' invitation is to not live in resignation but rather do the work of reconciliation out of a hope for healing and connection. There are no guarantees that it will end in the results you want, but it will always be an opening to soften your heart toward the other, and to lean deeper into empathy, love, and compassion for them as you engage in this process.

Our God is a God of love and reconciliation. He calls us to follow his example with one another.

For God was in Christ, reconciling the world to himself, no longer counting people's sins against them. And he gave us this wonderful message of reconciliation. For God made Christ, who never sinned, to be the offering for our sin, . . . so that we could be made right with God through Christ. **2 Corinthians 5:19, 21 (NLT)**

It is never too late to pursue reconciliation whether you have been hurt or the one who created the hurt. To do so invites you into the very work of Christ. This has the potential to rewrite your future and transform your legacy.

PERSONAL STUDY NOTES

SCRIPTURE REFLECTION

PERSONAL STUDY QUESTIONS

1. What relationship(s) do you currently have that are in need of reconciliation? What can you do to move toward that possibility?

2. Do you have a parent you desire a more open, connected relationship with? Or perhaps a child? What first steps can you take toward reconciling that relationship?

3. Forgiveness can be achieved even when parents have passed away. In that case, you work on your relationship toward them in your heart and mind. Take notice of where you hold unforgiveness. Are you willing to start doing the sacred work of forgiving? Can you release them from the desire that they pay for the pain they caused you? This can be deeply challenging. It does cost you something. Draw courage from the truth that your forgiveness cost Jesus everything.

4. Have I addressed my action step that I shared with my CORE group? If not, what is keeping me from stepping out and addressing it? What's my next step?

SCRIPTURE REFLECTION PRACTICE

We encourage you to consider the following Scripture passage over the course of this week in a prayerfully contemplative way. This simple process will help you engage not only your mind but also your heart. Consider focusing this week on the same Scripture below (Colossians 3:12–16) each day, using these principles:

- Be alert for a phrase or word that catches your attention. This could be in the form of a question on what it means or a new insight.
- Once during the week, read the verse aloud slowly.
- Once during the week, as you read the verses, pause along the way to use it to spark specific prayers to God.
- Finally, after reading the verses, pause to be thankful that, *"it is God who works in you, both to will and to work for his good pleasure."* **Philippians 2:13 (ESV)**

SCRIPTURE REFLECTION FOR SESSION 4: COLOSSIANS 3:12–16 (ESV)

Put on then, as God's chosen ones, holy and beloved, compassionate hearts, kindness, humility, meekness, and patience, bearing with one another and, if one has a complaint against another, forgiving each other; as the Lord has forgiven you, so you also must forgive.

And above all these put on love, which binds everything together in perfect harmony. And let the peace of Christ rule in your hearts, to which indeed you were called in one body. And be thankful.

Let the word of Christ dwell in you richly, teaching and admonishing one another in all wisdom, singing psalms and hymns and spiritual songs, with thankfulness in your hearts to God.

SCRIPTURE REFLECTION NOTES

PURPOSE

TOM PATERSON

GROUP DISCUSSION GUIDE 90 MINUTES

OPENING PRAYER

Surrender your time and heart to God's leading.

CHECK IN (20 MINUTES)

Be mindful that you are not taking more time to talk than the others in the group.

1. How has your week gone? Family? Work?

2. What kind of progress or challenges did you have with your "Next Step" from last session?

3. How was your Personal Study and Scripture Reflection time this week? What is resonating? What is not working?

Check In time is high on encouragement and low on "accountability."

WATCH FILM (13 MINUTES)
Purpose—Tom Paterson

GROUP DISCUSSION (45 MINUTES)

1. Which part of Tom's story or what Pete (the narrator for this film) shared connected with you?

2. What are you most clear about regarding your purpose?

3. Pete said once we are settled in knowing our identity as God's son, we can be free to live out our divine purpose. How do you think that idea would impact you and your purpose?

NEXT STEPS (10 MINUTES)

Be mindful of the need for everyone to have an opportunity to talk. Take 2–3 minutes each. Take notes and pray for each other's action steps during the week. As always, keep everything confidential.

In light of today's discussion, what is one step you can take in your life or in your relationships this week? Something specific. Something measurable. Something the group can pray for during the week.

PERSONAL STUDY EXCERPT—READ OUT LOUD (2 MINUTES)

Brotherhood is a primary component in working your way through the fog of uncertainty. As Pete unpacks in the film, "There is power in a well-timed question, that cuts through all the fog and allows the good, bad, and ugly around that question to come out and be made visible. It's hard to do this alone. It's because we need help. We need brothers, friends who believe deeply in us, are willing to listen, and are curious about what's wrong. What's confused? What's missing? Where am I failing? Where am I succeeding? And they give us hope. Otherwise, all there is, is judgment. We don't need more judgment. We judge ourselves harshly enough. Sometimes just getting that stuff out of my head and heart begins to bring hope in a bizarre way."

CLOSING PRAYER

Ask for God's guidance and strength during the week ahead.

THE SECRET OF MAN'S BEING IS NOT ONLY TO LIVE – BUT TO LIVE FOR SOMETHING DEFINITE.

CORE GROUP NOTES

⊕ PERSONAL STUDY

Tom Patterson has lived an amazing life. He's experienced success, achievement, and notoriety. He has also endured great tragedy, overwhelming loss, personal failure, addiction, and marital struggle— all this in one package.

Personal loss, tragedy, and failure do not disqualify you from being a vibrant participant in God's purpose for you.

Tom Paterson's protégé, Pete Richardson, mentions, "Most men lead lives of quiet desperation and die with the song still in their heart." That quote is usually attributed to author David Thoreau.

Here is Thoreau's full quote from the 1800s:

"The mass of men lead lives of quiet desperation. What is called resignation is confirmed desperation. . . A stereotyped but unconscious despair is concealed even under what are called the games and amusements of mankind."

Even though Thoreau said this over 150 years ago, it still rings true today.

God's calling pierces this nagging fear of desperation, isolation, and meaninglessness. He has a specific, unique calling and purpose for everyone, including you.

In Genesis, He states clearly that His intention is for us to collaborate with Him to be fruitful and multiply and subdue the earth **(Genesis 1:28)**. This vision is to develop the social order and harness the natural world. The result God is after is universal flourishing. The amazing thing is that he wants to work through you to help others thrive.

God's original intent has been to collaborate with us in order to create cultures, build civilizations, and harness nature as we reflect His image of love, righteousness, and goodness.

Our grand, overarching purpose is to collaborate with God and others to create flourishing, wholeness, and delight—in your personal life, your family life, your work life, your faith life, and your community life.

As Pete Richardson says, "When I think you see the big picture of life from birth to death, we realize how fast life is. Life is quick. It's swift. It's a blade of grass—green today, brown tomorrow—blown away by the wind the day after. To see your life as a gift and to begin to live day in and day out in gratitude for that gift—and using your giftedness to make the world better in some way—I think that's purpose."

You have your story. Those in your CORE group have their story. But your story does not define you. As Pete says:

"The thing with story is that any good story has its pinnacle times of great happiness and everything is going well and then deep dark valleys of hopelessness. The human story can be paralyzing if certain dots aren't connected. I know in my own story, some events in my life felt like outliers. They felt like disconnected, unmeaningful episodes . . . many of which I wish I could have deleted or erased. But what I discovered is that there's never a meaningless experience or episode in your life."

The reason for this is that God redeems the losses and failures for His purposes, if we allow Him to. He uses our seasons of sorrow to bring us closer to Him, His grace, and His mercy. The second beatitude says: *"Blessed are they who mourn, for they will be comforted"* **(Matthew 5:4)**. Pain and suffering can either drive us away from God as we seek to disconnect from the pain through addictions and distractions, or it can draw us closer to God, as we pursue His comfort, His grace, and His mercy.

Choosing to rest in His grace and mercy is a path that ultimately leads to a new perspective, joy, and restoration. It is in this transformational process that our specific call and purpose can be refined. The foundation of this is being freed from guilt and shame. And becoming confident in what God believes is true about us.

Pete mentions how Jesus began His ministry on earth with His Father affirming that He loves Him and is pleased with Him. And in the same way, the Scriptures address how we are to get settled with the truth that, *"You received God's Spirit when he adopted you as his own children. Now we call him, 'Abba Father.' For his Spirit joins with our spirit to affirm we are God's children."* **Romans 8:15–16 (NLT)**

One of the primary works of the Holy Spirit in our lives is to affirm that we are beloved sons. Only when we understand the truth that not only have we been forgiven, but that we are adopted and empowered sons, will we stop seeking the false idols of the broken male culture to give us satisfaction. This is as big a battle as you will ever face in your life. That's why we need the help of brothers to remind us of who we really are and what we were made for.

Brotherhood is a primary component in working your way through the fog of uncertainty. As Pete unpacks in the film, "There is power in a well-timed question that cuts through all the fog and allows the good, bad, and ugly around that question to come out and be made visible. It's hard to do this alone. It's because we need help.

"We need brothers, friends who believe deeply in us and are willing to listen and are curious about what's wrong. What's confused? What's missing? Where am I failing? Where am I succeeding? And they give us hope. Otherwise, all there is, is judgment. We don't need more judgment. We judge ourselves harshly enough. Sometimes just getting that stuff out of my head and heart begins to bring hope in a bizarre way."

Clarifying your specific purpose is an ongoing unveiling. Interaction within your group can help pierce the fog of subjectivity that we all have **(1 Corinthians 13:12)** through the input and example of others. We also need others to encourage us when we can't see the impact our lives are having or could have. They help us see God's hand as He guides us out of the wildernesses of our own making.

The key is to be willing to step out of the familiar and into new expressions of serving others. Become open to this grand calling. Be curious about what God has been preparing you for. Be intentional to put yourself in opportunities to create flourishing for others.

They may not seem like grand, earthshaking arenas. Just be willing to step out. God knows how to direct and redirect you as long as you are moving. He will hone your awareness of new ways you can contribute to the magnificent vision of His kingdom come, His will be done, on earth as it is in heaven.

PERSONAL STUDY NOTES

SCRIPTURE REFLECTION

PERSONAL STUDY QUESTIONS

1. What are you clear about right now regarding God's purpose for you?

2. Specifically, what areas of flourishing in the world and your life are you currently called to? What are you passionate about? What do you love? How have you seen God use you?

3. Have I addressed my "Next Steps" that I shared with my CORE group? If not, what is keeping me from stepping out and addressing it?

SCRIPTURE REFLECTION PRACTICE

We encourage you to consider the following Scripture passage over the course of this week in a prayerfully contemplative way. This simple process will help you engage not only your mind but also your heart. Consider focusing this week on the same Scripture below (Romans 12:1–2) each day, using these principles:

- Be alert for a phrase or word that catches your attention. This could be in the form of a question on what it means or a new insight.
- Once during the week, read the verses aloud slowly.
- Once during the week, as you read the verses, pause along the way to use it to spark specific prayers to God.
- Finally, after reading the verses, pause to be thankful that, *"it is God who works in you, both to will and to work for his good pleasure."* **Philippians 2:13 (ESV)**

SCRIPTURE REFLECTION FOR SESSION 5: ROMANS 12:1–2 (ESV)

I appeal to you therefore, brothers, by the mercies of God, to present your bodies as a living sacrifice, holy and acceptable to God, which is your spiritual worship. Do not be conformed to this world, but be transformed by the renewal of your mind, that by testing you may discern what is the will of God, what is good and acceptable and perfect.

SCRIPTURE REFLECTION NOTES

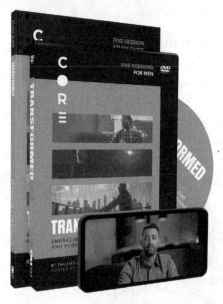

EMBRACING OUR TRUE IDENTITY AND PURPOSE

God never designed us to just figure things out on our own. When Jesus came to earth to start a revolution, he did so by gathering a small band of ordinary men around him. These men had unique backgrounds, diverse occupations, and individual personalities. Jesus orchestrated learning environments as they worked alongside each other that changed them into the most powerful transformative community in the history of the word. Together, they went from self-centered individuals to united powerhouses.

Study Guide: 9780310131755
DVD with Free Streaming Access: 9780310131779

The goal of the CORE studies is set men on a similar journey that will transform them and their group into this type of community. Each study features five real-life stories of men who have faced real-life challenges and discovered transformation, redemption, restoration, purpose, and identity. These stories serve as a catalyst for men to start being real about their own stories.and realize they are not alone in the struggle. In turn, this opens them up to getting the encouragement necessary to engage in life proactively.

There has never been a more critical need to equip men with the tools to win the battles over their hearts and futures. CORE gives them the ability to create spaces where they can show up as they are without judgment, be open about their struggles, and find freedom to discover who God says they are. They will be invited to step out of shame and isolation and encouraged to step into their God-given purpose.

This study features an introduction from Jeremy Affeldt and stories from well-known speakers on the topics of identity, transformation, brotherhood, choices, and renewal.

Available now at your favorite bookstore,
or streaming video on StudyGateway.com.